LAUNCHING OUT
Christian Healing in Scotland

REMINISCENCES
by Rev J. Clarence Finlayson

LAUNCHING OUT
Christian Healing in Scotland

REMINISCENCES
by Rev J. Clarence Finlayson

First Published 1994

Produced by Challenger Resource, Edinburgh

The photograph of Rev Cameron Peddie from "The Forgotten Talent", courtesy of the publishers, Arthur James Ltd, 1 Cranbourne Road, London N10 2BT.

all Blessing
Florence Findlay

CONTENTS

FOREWORD

Anyone who stays with the Community on Iona for a week can't fail to come across the Healing Ministry. Every Tuesday, summer and winter, at the Evening Service in the Abbey, we pray for both individuals and communities by name, and share in the ministry of the laying on of hands. Scores of people are involved every week. And Iona, too, is the centre of a Prayer Circle of men and women, all over the world, who are committed, every week, to pray for people whose names are sent out by our Prayer Circle Secretary in the Abbey. She writes, and receives, literally hundreds of letters every month.

Guests often ask: Why Iona? What's so special about Iona? The best answer I ever heard was given by a visiting Anglican Bishop, himself a member of the Prayer circle. "I send names here" he said, "not because Iona itself is special but because I know that, over the years, week in week out, there are people living here who are committed to the work of wholeness and healing, in their life-style as well as in their prayer".

The story of the Healing Ministry of the Iona Community is the story, not the success, but rather of discipleship - of following, of faithfulness, of failure and of forgiveness. It is part of a much wider story too: of a growing awareness that this Ministry is part and parcel of the Ministry of all God's people: that healing and wholeness are to do with political and social action every bit as much as with personal love and prayer, and the skill of all in the medical and caring professions.

Clarence Finlayson is rightly regarded, with much affection, as one of the pioneers in the recovery of this Ministry in Scotland in our times. His own journey of discipleship, recorded here, richly deserves to be read. It will strengthen and encourage many; it will undoubtedly disturb others: I do not think any will be able to read it without recognising the work of the Holy Spirit. For us in the Iona community, what he has to say reminds us of our roots, and calls us to greater faithfulness: so for telling it as it was, we are most grateful.

Rev. John Harvey,

Leader of the Iona Community.
Iona - Palm Sunday 1989

INTRODUCTION

The reason for my writing this story is simply to put on record the early years of the main stream Healing Ministry in Scotland, for there are so few of us now who can go back some forty years, that there is danger of all being forgotten.

In setting about the task it is inevitable that one should view things from one's own particular angle. I suppose that at times I have tended to be cautious as, remembering that in this modern age we have about us the experience and devotion of those professionally trained in dealing with bodily ailments, there is a need to keep credulity under control. But I believe there is a spiritual dimension where also there is much to be explored. The first thing, however, is to gather facts. Verdicts can come later.

Over the years my own views have changed slightly, some might say matured, but belief in the reality of the Healing Ministry is still vital to my thinking. One afternoon recently while waiting at a bus stop on the outskirts of the city, I found there a young man, who, seeing my clerical collar informed me that he himself was a candidate for the ministry. He came straight to the point which was exercising his mind "If you were starting again would you still choose the same career?" I hope he recognised the sincerity of my reply when I responded "If I had to choose again there is nothing else which would enter my mind!" Over the years, of course, there have been rebuffs and even doubts, but being engaged in the Master's service and given a chance to help others gives one a sense of fulfilment which is abundantly satisfying. Along conventional lines one might still have felt this to be true, but I can only say that as far as I myself am concerned the realisation that the kind of healing portrayed in the New Testament is still valid today, has brought to my own ministry much greater depth, and one hopes that setting this down in permanent form may be of value to others who still have years of service ahead.

BEGINNINGS

Perhaps I might begin the story with my own early personal contacts with Healing before the Second World War. Up to this time one can safely say that it had no place at all in Scottish Church life, and one regarded its manifestations as belonging to the realms of the sects.

But two experiences came my way when holidaying in England. Being interested in the activities centred in Headingley where a gentleman named Bradman was showing his prowess, I found myself in Leeds. Here I obtained Bed and Breakfast facilities from a lady whom I heard announcing to her family in a loud, rather startled voice "We've got a parson!"

However she was not over- abashed, for one evening she took me to the mid-week service of her imposing Christian Science Church. At this several people recounted healing experiences they had recently had. Any impression made on me was, I fear, largely superficial. This denomination produces many fine people and I hold it in high respect, yet I did not feel it's approach would be very helpful in my own ministry as it seemed to demand standards culturally and intellectually beyond the man in the street.

By a strange coincidence the following week while I was in York it turned out that my hostess again was involved in the Healing Ministry. Mrs Welman herself immediately impressed one as being a person of unusual gifts. She told me a strange tale. One day, several years before, on looking out from the bedroom window she had suddenly seen her invalid daughter's funeral cortege exactly as she was to perceive it in reality some weeks later! She herself suffered from acute deafness, and hearing that a local spiritualist society were interested in healing it is not surprising that she became one of their members. But the hoped-for cure did not come and when a Pentecostal Church set up in York she transferred to them and claimed that her hearing was restored as she accepted their faith. It was with some anticipation that I accepted her invitation to their mid-week service and there I was introduced to their minister. Alas! The service did not attract me. Emotionalism was worked up to a degree I felt repelling and though cures were claimed around me I felt this was certainly not the way for me. And that was the end of any interest I might have in Healing for many years to come.

It is strange, however, and so unfortunate, how the Church has, down the years neglected this side of its challenge. Reading the Gospels we ought surely to recognise that from the beginning of His own Ministry Jesus combined healing with preaching. The Word manifested itself not just in converting but in healing. He dealt with the whole man, body, mind and spirit. Looking back on my early years in the ministry I am sure I could have been of much more use to my people had I known the wider and fuller approach.

In the succeeding post-war years I had charges first in Carntyne Old Church, Shettleston, in the east end of Glasgow and then in what was to become St James' in the new housing area of Pollok. At this time the main centre of religious activity was generated by the Iona Community which, in addition to the Abbey restoration on the island, had, in the city, its House on Clyde Street. The latter building had its residence on the top floor, a variety of rooms for meeting below, with on the ground, a large area for serving and partaking meals. In addition there was an adjoining space, un-divided from the rest, for daily services. In for a coffee or perhaps lunch, one often shared in a service and so was introduced to the practice of praying for the sick by name. Not that there was anything revolutionary about this, but it did give special point to prayers which are so often regarded as being only of devotional significance.

However, this may have helped to influence one in deciding to attend a class on Divine Healing to be addressed by a series of speakers with personal experience of the subject. Only two were known to me, Dr George MacLeod himself and Rev. Cameron Peddie, minister in Hutchesontown, who had gained a reputation for his work among the gangs in the Gorbals. Other speakers were mostly from south of the Border, some having had missionary experience mainly in India where the Healing Ministry had a strong hold from early in the century.

There would be over a dozen of us with Rev.Fred Smith as chairman as we gathered weekly round the table.

On the first evening I had travelled to the meeting by tram from Sauchiehall Street with, in the seat in front of me, two young ladies. We all got off together in Jamaica Street and, lo and behold! they turned up in due course round the table with the rest of us. One of them was Miss Kelso who had been a hospital nurse in London until war-time when a bomb exploding nearby had completely destroyed the hearing in one ear. This verdict was endorsed by the medical opinion that the organ had been so shattered that no medical or surgical treatment would be of any value in improving the condition. Miss Kelso's work was so affected by the impairment that she had had to give up her post in London and become a doctor's receptionist in Glasgow.

The purpose of the class was really educative. Healing then played so small a part in the life of the Church that it was hoped that a wide selection of different approaches to the subject would lead to its being taken seriously by the public. So, after we had had a number of speakers along conventionally religious lines,one night we were introduced to Mrs Lyons, Glasgow's best known "psychic". She had been a Roman Catholic but had been informed that she herself had healing powers after her son had been cured by somebody with a psychic approach. She thereafter embarked on Healing and recounted to us numerous cases where remarkable cures had been obtained. She concluded by saying that she regretted that she had not brought with her any of those who could have confirmed her claims but if there was anyone present in need she would be glad to see what she could do.

At this, Miss Kelso, who hitherto had taken little part in our discussion spoke up and told her story. Mrs Lyons thereupon laid her hands on Miss Kelso's head and, after a pause, announced that she thought the consultants were wrong. The damage was not very serious, only a nerve had been affected! The ladies conversed for a little and then Miss Kelso said "You don't need to shout. I can hear you quite well!" Her hearing had been restored, and she departed from the meeting a happy and somewhat astonished woman. I may say that Miss Kelso and her friend did not return to the class but some months later she told me that the cure had been permanent and she had returned to nursing.

The episode, which attracted much publicity at the time, raises several questions. First of all it comes as a challenge. Has not the Church been neglecting an important part of its New Testament heritage and been not very diligent in trying to regain it? This is why Cameron Peddie entitled his book "The Forgotten Talent". Then again, one wonders whether Healing is not a natural gift possessed by many though in differing degrees. Such would seem to have been the accepted view in St Paul's time (I Corinthians 12:28-30). There are indeed those who, though a needy person had been delivered from an encumbrance, condemn the proceedings because of the cult professed. Such might remember what was said of the heathen King Cyrus (Isaiah 45:4) "I have called thee... though thou hast not known my name." If conventional channels fail God often uses other means. In any case it is obvious that some strange insight was present when Mrs Lyons was audacious enough to contradict the professionals' diagnosis before the healing took place. There seem indeed to be more things in heaven and earth than are dreamt of by mere materialists. It is interesting that nowadays there is so much excitement, in Moscow of all places, at the cures being recorded by a professional healer functioning through television!

THE GLASOW GROUP

Under Fred Smith's guidance there was formed a ministers' group, meeting each Monday afternoon, and this was to be the spearhead of the new movement throughout Scotland. Fred himself was an Englishman with contacts south of the Border and we were surprised how long Spiritual healing had been established there, not only in the Churches but in various societies and healing homes. Canterbury itself had given this aspect of the faith its blessing, co-operating with many of the highest figures in medicine, the Methodist, Dr Leslie Weatherhead of the City Temple in London had made a major contribution to the subject. It has to be said that not just on our own island but in the United States where the movement also is strong the Anglican Church had been the main cradle of Divine Healing. From this of course we in Scotland found not only new friends but a new source of life and energy for our ministry. These Mondays at Community House were full of interest as we welcomed instructed visitors and discussed new ideas. Our membership was not limited to clerics. Laymen appeared in our ranks and a few doctors evinced considerable interest. On one occasion we ventured afield and spent some time on the island of Iona where in the Community we had our devotional life deepened in that ancient centre of Healing.

It is interesting how most new movements follow a similar pattern in their development. So, after the period we spent really studying the subject and in fellowship absorbing it, the time came when we felt we must put this new aspect of the ministry into practice and hold services monthly in one another's churches. It may seem strange to some people nowadays that one of the first questions that this venture raised was that of publicity. Should not such services, for fear of sensationalism be private? This is an indication of how novel the whole thing was in Scotland at the time. But not very much later, at least for major events, we not only permitted but invited the attention of the press. It is interesting that Jesus Himself at first requested those whom He had healed not to tell others, but that eventually He too accepted the situation and expressed surprise that some people did not believe though with their own eyes they had seen His wonderful work. It seems that when people become accustomed to an occurrence they soon take it for granted and cease to wonder. Perhaps we should be pleased when Healing is today regarded as part of the normal Christian ministry.

REV. CAMERON PEDDIE

As will become evident from the record a great deal of the progress we made in understanding and developing the Ministry of Healing in Glasgow was due to the influence of Rev. Cameron Peddie whose story is well recounted in his autobiography "The Forgotten Talent". As our group met weekly for discussion and prayer it was he who made the subject live and he who in due course encouraged us to put it into practice. He was God's special agent in our particular situation.

Perhaps for me personally the first major event was when together we visited one of my members suffering severely from the lung disease known as emphysema. The latter was an engineer in the underground railway, but though only in his forties had for many weeks been off work confined to the house and extremely ill. The doctor had informed him that little could be done to alleviate the condition and that he must resign himself to being more or less confined to the house. He did not impress me as being a specially religious man and looking at him, a rather forlorn figure sitting there somewhat breathless, I confess I did not really anticipate much change before we left. Peddie, however, proceeded with his ministrations placing hands on his chest back and front. After a few minutes he asked him if he felt anything special. At first there was no reply and then he said "Yes! There is something happening. I feel it going right through me!" Then suddenly with eyes almost popping out of his head he gasped to his wife "I'm better! I'm better!" Into my mind flashed the words of Jesus "Many have longed to see this day and have not seen it. But blessed are your eyes for they see and your ears for they hear!"

That there was healing, there was little doubt as in a few days the sick man was able to take the considerable walk round the block where he lived and in the weeks ahead gradually regained his strength. Eventually he decided to return to his work and, as he preferred to do so on the night-shift, I sometimes saw him waiting at the bus stop on a foggy winter evening and conveyed him by car to the nearest underground station. But we knew the cure was not complete for he took severe attacks of illness when we might be called to help. Indeed the family used to be amused when the schoolboy son would say "Will I go and get not the doctor but the minister?" One attack, however, came on suddenly and with such severity that it was too late for any help to be given. What the clinical verdict on the patient had been through all this we do not know but all concerned would claim that some form of healing had been at work.

The circumstances through which I myself came to be involved in Peddie's work was that when our group decided to hold their monthly service in St James' I asked him if he would be willing to visit those of my members unable to come to the church. To this he agreed with the addendum that he would come three times if I agreed thereafter to carry on by myself! From these visits, of course, I learned a great deal. There were complete cures which I shall be outlining in future pages but God deals with different people in different ways and in apparently differing degrees. Frequently what was hoped for was not achieved as we would have liked but nearly always there was something to think about. One good man with heart trouble did not

14

receive the easement he had been anticipating, but when he awoke on the following day he found that a finger bent into the palm of his hand from childhood had gone straight. As he philosophically commented "There must have been some healing working inside me!" In another case we went to see a woman housebound with disseminated sclerosis and found, at home with her, her husband, a lorryman who had to lift heavy loads and had so strained himself that he was quite unable to go to his work. It was he, rather than his wife, who received the healing. He returned to his work next day and, many months later, was completely fit, the envy of his mate always complaining of his aches and pains. But how off-hand about God's work we can be is illustrated in the case of a man suffering so acutely from an ailment that he pled with me to obtain Mr Peddie's help. At considerable inconvenience the latter came and gave his ministry. Next day when I called round the pain had completely disappeared but all I got from the patient was "Oh, these are wonderful tablets!" There may be a lesson here for us all!

Behind his exercise of the Healing Ministry Cameron Peddie had of course a deeply devotional life. Indeed he had years of earnest seeking before it became obvious that he himself was to become a pioneer in the spread of this approach. It was, over many years, his custom every evening, as nearly as circumstances permitted, to spend the hour before midnight in prayer and meditation. I was privileged to share in this with him during a whole week when we together visited Milton Abbey, Dorset, then a Home for Healing. Each evening we repaired to the side chapel there, a room with large windows looking out on the lawns, at midsummer admitting considerable twilight. There we meditated in peaceful contemplation along normal lines. But on our last night he said to me "This is too bright. Let us go into the main chapel - originally the monks' refectory - where it is much darker." This we did and in a short time one became very conscious indeed of the unseen world closing in upon us. At first it was helpful enough in one's meditation, but eventually it became so oppressive that I said "I don't like this!" To which my companion replied "If you won't wait, God won't speak to you!" However I must confess that I was so scared that the episode was abruptly terminated and we retired to our rooms. Next morning Peddie was serene and uplifted and he told me that after we had separated God had come specially near him. For myself I can only say that one has to be taken through an experience like this to know the reality of another world beyond.

That Cameron Peddie had exceptional spiritual insight I was reminded again and again. One day he received a telephone call from a doctor in a hospital just outside the city. The latter's wife, in the later stages of a malignant disease was suffering severe pain and had expressed a strong desire to have his help. If the doctor sent a car would Mr Peddie be willing to meet her request? Peddie agreed and said "I will keep her in my prayers until the car arrives". The first visit was succeeded by others over the three remaining weeks of the patient's life, during which drugs were discontinued and the pain subsided. The doctor expressed his gratitude and said "I wish most sincerely to thank you for what you did and also for the fact that over these weeks you gave me back my wife." To this Peddie replied "There's just one thing puzzles me. Before I had been here at all and while I was waiting for your car to arrive and was engaged in seeking God's blessing on my visit I could visualise your wife quite clearly but in a room quite different from where I've seen her." The doctor looked astonished and said "But that wasn't the room she was in when I telephoned" and taking him across the landing opened a door and showed Peddie a room exactly as he had seen it in his prayers. So, what to the casual eye might have seemed just a series of visits by an elderly minister saying comforting prayers, revealed itself as possessing a different dimension.

Many of those engaged in spiritual healing are aware that associated with it are physical reactions mostly, on the part of those being treated but occasionally by the minister himself. Peddie said he was always conscious of what he called the power being switched on and then off. Most of us, I fear, are insensitive to this experience.

But with those receiving the ministry it is a fairly common occurrence. There was one strange case when an elderly man who, though he got considerable relief from his symptoms yet himself knew that he had not far to go, was visited by Peddie and one of our group. After a few visits together the patient was left on his own but always with the treatment went not only relief but strong sensations of heat experienced by the invalid. On one crucial night, however, not heat but extreme cold was felt, and though our member heated his hands to ensure that he himself was not the cause, it was of no avail. Nonetheless the patient otherwise seemed none the worse, and later that evening having enjoyed a good meal he settled down comfortably. Some hours later however he passed away. The family always maintained that there was a connection between the two events.

But there is no doubt that strange reactions were a more regular feature with Peddie than most of us. On one occasion when ministering the laying on of hands he bent over and placing his hand on the sole of the house-shoe of the invalid asked him if he experienced any reaction. The latter did not immediately reply but then said "I was wondering if it was the heat of the fire!" It was with the same man and in similar circumstances that Peddie extended his hand and I observed in it a measurable depth of liquid. "The Lord provides His own oil!" was his comment.Later, he remarked that this happened to him, from time to time, and that sometimes there was a sweet odour. I tended to regard this as pious imagination until there came into my hands a recently published book entitled "The Reluctant Healer" by an American W. J. MacMillan, in which the author claimed that a similar occurrence happened to him sometimes to his considerable embarrassment. As these two men never, at that time anyway, had even heard of one another there must surely be here something more than coincidence.

It was, of course, not surprising that being in touch with these things one should find greater depth in one's own ministry. This was illustrated in two events which came my way in these early days and seemed, apart from their own value, to serve the purpose of encouraging me myself to go forward in faith.

The first was not specially surprising since it occurred in my normal visiting when in one house the housewife was ill and in bed. We talked about Mr Peddie's work and before leaving I ministered to the lady offering healing prayers. When I had gone she announced she was feeling quite well, got up and proceeded with her normal duties. When I heard the story afterwards it was its very unspectacular nature which most impressed me.

The other event was very different. One Sunday morning arriving at the church I found on the vestry table a letter from the Boys' Brigade Captain, "William George (14), Lynbank Avenue, is seriously ill in the Southern General Hospital with tubercular peritonitis. The doctors say there is no hope of recovery. The boy does not know how ill he is."

The boy's home was outside our parish and I did not know the family, but on the Tuesday I went round to the house. When the mother saw me at the garden gate she feared the worst as the usual sequence is doctor, minister, undertaker! However I assured her that I was not the bearer of bad news, but that if she cared to accompany me in my car we could go to the hospital together. To this she agreed and on our way I told her of my healing experiences but said I was not sure if the hospital would be very keen on my approach. To this she replied "Oh they will have no objection as they have told me they can do no more." So indeed, it turned out and the nurses were most co-operative. I explained to William the purpose of my visit and gave him a service. Though I myself saw no change his mother always maintained he from that time took a turn for the better. Mr Peddie accompanied me on a further visit. We sat on either side of the bed with our hands on the boy's body. After some minutes my friend asked him if he felt anything happening. At first there was no reply but on the question being repeated the boy said "It's gone now!" What this meant we did not know but we concluded the service and I was much relieved, for William looked so ill that I felt he might pass out there and then.

Really concerned I went round to the house late in the evening to see how the mother had got on when she had called at the usual visiting hour, and was informed that she had not yet returned from another visit in Govan since. So on Friday I went once again to hear what the news might be and, I confess, I was full of foreboding. I need not have worried. When she saw my car stop she threw her door open and greeted me with a welcoming smile "William is so much better" she said and she unfolded a strange story. When she and a neighbour had entered the ward William was sitting up combing his hair and asking for a stronger comb. Then he said "I had a strange experience this afternoon. The ministers came and put their hands on me and I felt as if my whole body was full of oil! I feared I might be sick in front of them, but the sensation, after gathering in my chest went down and circulated in my stomach, then down my legs and out through the soles of my feet. Since then I've been fine!" And so it was. He was transferred to a convalescent hospital and eventually discharged to live a normal life. With these experiences behind me I was well launched on a ministry in which Christian healing was to have an important part.

ST JAMES (POLLOK)

In the circumstances here, we were well favoured in developing a new approach. Pollok was a new housing estate with a population within our parish boundaries of some 20,000 people. I was inducted there in 1948 though there was then neither congregation nor church building. We began with Sunday services in an infant schoolroom, graduating as far as accommodation was concerned by hut and permanent halls until, after five years we came into possession of a very fine church which had been transported stone by stone from another part of the city. Our people came largely from the inner city but proved themselves a fine responsible community looking expectantly forward to building for themselves a prosperous future and creating a strong congregation. A good proportion, who became founder members of St James' had been members back in the city for in the industrial areas the church played a valuable part not only in providing Sunday worship but, on weekdays, a happy and healthy social life for both young and old. But there were others who felt it easier to be connected with the less socially-demanding missions. The latter have not had a good press and have sometimes even been caricatured by the ignorant. I am glad to have this opportunity of saying that my own experience has been that these missions, in the days and conditions in which they found themselves, did a splendid job both in maintaining morale and in inculcating high moral standards. In St James' we were glad to admit to full membership many people who previously, because of their circumstances, had not found it possible to submit to the formal ritual. Indeed, in six years St James' grew to be one of the largest congregations in the city - but its main feature was its fine spirit. Furthermore people looking expectantly to the future were always open to new ideas and never said "We never did this before" when fresh proposals were made!

So the ideas behind the Healing Ministry were readily accepted. Yet I have always felt that new proposals in a congregation's life, should have official backing and the matter was thus fully discussed by and had the full backing of the Kirk Session. Thus instead of I, myself, being mainly responsible for advancing the cause, the

movement became, part of Church routine shared by all. Many things went on, unreported to me. Going through my papers in sorting out the material for this record, I have just come across this portion of a letter received long since:

"Dear Mr Finlayson

I know you will be delighted to hear the good news about Pat. The heart specialist says her heart has healed. She no longer needs any drugs, and she can start going to an ordinary school. He says it is a miracle. I can hardly believe it after seven years of worrying and watching her every move. It is seven years since we first brought her to your Church for Faith Healing. I'll never forget the sore heart I had the first time I brought her as we were so sure it was pretty hopeless. I only wish her Dad was living to know about this, as the doctors and everyone else who knows Pat are amazed. She has not to take PT. in school for about six months, but otherwise she can lead a normal life. Pat is coming along on Sunday morning to your church....."

We shall be considering in a later chapter what may be the clinical assessment of such cases. Here one would just comment that the kind of spiritual atmosphere it assumes seems far nearer that of the New Testament story than the sometimes cold and alienating one of the merely formal or predominantly theological church.

The Kirk Session agreed with me that the Healing should not be restricted to the work of the minister alone and that the whole congregation should be involved. Nor did they think it should be left to small groups however loyal and devoted, but that even the simplest had a part to play and might themselves grow in knowledge and grasp of the faith. So we organised an Intercessory Service as part of ordinary Sunday worship. For several reasons we chose to have it as an addendum to the evening service at 6.30 to 7.30. Though smaller than the morning services we still had regular attendances well into three figures in the evening and most people were content to wait on for the extra fifteen minutes to which we strictly limited the time of the Intercessory. Some waited perhaps because it was easier than to rise up and go, some because they were curious, and some because they were desperately in earnest. There were even some who came because of the Intercessory and I well recall a Roman Catholic family attending regularly because we were remembering one of their number, something for which their own Church made no provision.

Something those engaged in Spiritual Healing soon discover is that while in our secular age there is a falling off in those interested in the faith conventionally presented, one is almost embarrassed by the enthusiasm of response when it is connected with Healing. Thus when we intimated that our prayers would include the names of all given to us we found ourselves, like others, in difficulty in dealing adequately with the numbers we had. One missioner from overseas to whom I mentioned the problem said airily "Oh, don't worry about that! Just mention the names in your list. God knows their identity and their need." But one might here reply "If it is as easy as that, why mention them at all?" As I myself had been learning, it seemed to me that vagueness and doing things by rote were just what we had to be wary of in our prayers. Intercession <u>must</u> be personal, caring and costly, which meant that numbers had to be restricted. So it was necessary to divide our list into four categories. First we remembered by name those seriously ill and then similarly new names submitted. Thirdly for individual intercession came those in one group according to their type of illness. Finally the others had to be grouped together in the Family List covered by an inclusive prayer until their turn came on some succeeding Sunday.

This "Intercessory" came to draw us together as few other sides of our busy church did! "My mother is going into hospital tomorrow. Will you put her name on the list tonight!" said a lad in the choir in the most natural way possible. "We're going parish visiting this coming week and are very nervous about it. Will you remember all like us?" was the request of one so engaged. Truly we were conscious of all being one in Christ Jesus. And the practice spread, as when one of our members asked us to include her daughter Margaret, who was a patient at a rather distant sanitorium, suffering from tuberculosis, this wasting disease, which until recent years, carried away great numbers of people, especially the young. Soon we heard that Margaret herself was keeping 7.30 to 7.45 with us; then that the whole ward was keeping it too and finally the whole hospital!

It was also inevitable that all branches of congregational life should be affected. On Thursday afternoons we had a Women's Meeting to which came news that Mrs R, after the birth of her baby was suffering such severe haemorrhage that her life was endangered. The usual order of meeting was thereupon abandoned and all concentrated on praying for this member. On learning the situation I went at once to the hospital and seeing her white and motionless, of course, offered prayer. Next day I returned and found that improvement had set in. Somehow the medical staff became aware of our special interest, for the consultant went out of his way to discuss the matter with me. He said "Her recovery is quite momentous." And though the entire medical staff had directed special attention on the patient with expert skill it was obvious that he had appreciated that more than normal factors had been at work.

God's ways, of course, are not our ways and healing may be of many kinds as the following story shows. One Sunday morning when I arrived at the church there was an urgent message awaiting from a family living immediately across the road asking if I would baptise the eldest son of the house, aged about thirty, who was in the last stage of tuberculosis. There had been a "mixed marriage" and though the children had been sent to a Catholic school there had been no definite commitment with any church. Since I myself was involved in our morning service, our Assistant went over and administered the sacrament as required there and then.

It so happened that we had in Glasgow that week-end Rev. William Wood of the London Healing Mission, officiating that morning in Paisley, but, prior to our own evening worship, we went together to minister to the dying man. While the family were most grateful he himself made virtually no comment.

We had a full congregation that evening, and when it came to the Intercessory Service I unfolded to them the tragedy of this young man so nearby, so struck down at the time of life usually considered its most vigorous period. As we prayed the atmosphere seemed so spiritually charged as to be almost tangible and one felt as if indeed a measure of healing was conveyed. And he did recover sufficiently to be removed to a hospital on the city outskirts. There I visited him several times. He had a room to himself but when I called the last time it was evident that the end was near. After I had prayed as usual he made initially no comment and I was leaving the room disappointed not only in the evident imminent outcome of his illness but in the fact that the impression that our prayers had been having some beneficial effect had been ill founded, when he *did* speak, making the first significant remark I had heard from him. He said "Thank you Father (the Catholic bit) for all you've done for me!" and I knew that God had indeed been working and brought peace to his soul.

COUNSELLING

Most ministers and many active Christians are asked from time to time to give counsel to someone in need. There are those who deliberately avoid this appeal and others who are scared, but it can often be the most valuable sphere of Christian service. Pollok, like similar areas at the time, provided a real challenge for here, though people were cut off from old ways of living. the general moral tone was high. I used to marvel that one of our ministerial assistants used to leave his open sports car at the church gate with on the shelf bars of chocolate, which could easily have been snatched up by a passer-by. But this never seemed to happen! Indeed there was a fair amount of juvenile delinquency at least partly due to the fact that we were miles from the city and its entertainments. The Community Centre at the time was outside our parish, there were no playing fields and our church's organisations provided almost the only provision for young people to occupy their leisure time. One year I found myself no fewer than twelve times defending mainly young people on mainly minor charges. The authorities were nearly always so glad to have ministers taking an active concern in the social problems of their parishioners that they were usually content to leave the matter with them. The Christian ministry has many sides but surely among the most important is to create the relationship in which people feel they can trust their minister. There was in my own experience a period when I knew I was being used by a young scallywag when he would come round and ask me after periods of truanting to take him back to school so that he might avoid punishment - as he always did! But I knew that behind his misbehaviour was a disturbed background, and it may have been that having received help over what might have been a disastrous adolescence, he was helped later to enjoy a happy marriage.

In Pollok one had a special opportunity to get alongside youngsters, but of course we have to be open to all ages. This is not always easy. I recall an occasion when a member said "Did you know that my neighbour is worrying greatly about a certain problem?"

I replied "No, and I think I could be of help. Why did she not ask me?" "That's just what I said to her" commented my informant "But she said 'O the minister is the last person I would want to know about it!'" One respects this attitude but surely to meet our people's need is the main responsibility of the ministry. Is not this what the word "minister" implies? The modern doctor and the lawyer often function in this capacity at a deeper level than their professions necessarily demand, and it is a great pity if the cleric is just a respectable figure on the fringe of real life. Nowadays we know that body, mind and spirit affect each other and one would not place too much value on the effectiveness of the efforts of those professing to bring healing along only one of these lines. To the paralytic youth, Jesus did not say "Get up and walk" until he had first said "Thy sins are forgiven thee." I would like it to be said of St James' that it had both a theological and a caring concern. At one time being on the Govan Committee of the Council of Social Service I contemplated there being a branch in our premises in St James'. I believe our parishioners would have thought this quite appropriate, for our members involved themselves in parish mission, visiting all homes within our bounds almost all the year round and the building itself stood for a centre of care and concern for the whole community. I remember a young woman stroking its walls and saying quietly to herself "How I love this Church!"

THE WIDER OUTLOOK

An undue portion of this survey of the early days of the Healing Movement in Scotland has been devoted to St James' Church (Pollok). Of course this is partly because it was here my own efforts were centred but, as we have explained, it provided conditions very conducive to a new venture. But other congregations in various ways were also introducing this ministry into their life. Thus an important charge in the city centre held a weekly service of healing which became widely known and was well attended. Paisley Abbey also became associated with this approach. Indeed, so quickly did the movement spread that the Glasgow Presbytery formed a committee to study and report on the matter. Before its work was finalised however, the General Assembly appointed a national committee to find its value for the whole country. The latter's report when it came out was somewhat non-committal for the subject was new and some of its members were reared in the belief that science alone held the key to the body's ills. This is a dilemma which frequently confronts most of us. Which will we go by - faith or reason? Today most people would say there is a place for both but a generation back many tended to be more cautious.

But the matter had been raised, the seed sown, and nowadays the Ministry of Healing, however understood - has become a respectable term in ecclesiastical vocabulary.

At the same time the contacts of our chairman, Frederick Smith, led to our Group's boundaries becoming greatly widened. The original impulse for taking seriously the Ministry of Christian Healing had been among Anglican missionaries in India in the opening years of the century so that in our time there were various groups and societies well established in England and the United States. We rapidly became familiar with certain of these and many of their leading figures paid us visits, sharing their experience and occupying our pulpits. So we took our place in a world-wide fellowship.

THE CHRISTIAN FELLOWSHIP
OF HEALING

When in 1961 I moved to Edinburgh to take up the charge of Grange Parish Church the main centre of Healing there was the Fellowship. But the circumstances here were quite different from those in Glasgow. The founder of the Fellowship had been Rev. J.A.C. Murray, minister of the Tolbooth Church and brother-in-law of Dr. George MacLeod. He had long had an active interest in Healing and was one of the leading members of the Guild of Health based in London. Naturally he was pleased at the Scottish spontaneity expressed in the Glasgow Group and he paid us a special visit to see if a body similiar to the various English societies might be formed north of the Border.

The suggestion, however, had a chilly reception. Cameron Peddie, in particular, held the view that such bodies tended to become 'oddities'. The Healing Ministry ought not to be regarded as a kind of optional feature for those inclined that way but part of the Church's normal life. But Mr Murray was a determined man, and he persuaded Peddie and Dr. Christopher Woodward (of "A Doctor Heals by Faith") to address a large public meeting in Edinburgh and from those present, secured sufficient enthusiasts to launch the present Christian Fellowship of Healing. His wife, one of the leading figures in the Girl's Guildry, collaborated with him and was instrumental in securing for him the necessary accommodation for the new body from her organisation. After a short period Mr Murray retired from his charge and was able to devote all his time to the Fellowship. Subsequently, however, his own health gave out and it seemed as if in the absence of an obvious clerical leader the hopes and plans of many interested people were about to come to an abrupt end.

Earlier this century when an example of Christian work sustained by faith was being sought, we in Scotland often pointed to the Orphan Homes at Bridge of Weir, founded and led by William Quarrier. No public appeal was ever made for finance yet for that great undertaking there was always sufficient for their needs. One day a reporter, wishing to write up the story was interviewing Quarrier in his office when a member of the staff entered with the news that the supply of potatoes had run out and there were none for that evening's supper. Quarrier said "We must pray about it!" - which they did. On leaving some time later the reporter was met at the gate by a farm worker leading in a cart loaded with the required vegetables! If we are really committed to God's work He does not fail. So, as we tell this story, it is worth noting that there are good grounds for seeing His hand, not only in our dealing with those seeking our help but in the development of the Fellowship itself.

Mr Murray, then, had made all arrangements for closing down the Fellowship and disposing of its funds, when the Committee, a group of splendid lay-people, met with him and were permitted to carry on. The contretemps coincided with my own arrival in Edinburgh and having been approached in the matter I agreed, if allowed an interim period for settling into my congregation, to act as chairman to the committee and give a limited time participating in its activities. Similarly, years later, the Fellowship being by this time well established, when one felt that way should be made for a younger leader, Ian Cowie with his unique gifts was available, and when, once again on his retirement, we wondered somewhat apprehensively where a successor might be found, how gratifying that Ian Davidson with much experience and deep knowledge of how to deal with people met our need so exactly. Similarly with accommodation, It was a daunting problem for a body with such limited resources,to find a home in a city centre. We had, successively, two sets of rooms in Ainslie Place and one in Coates Crescent. It was a sad day when we were informed that once again we must move! We were actually holding a special committee meeting, and had just concluded a special prayer for guidance, when the telephone beside us rang and we were informed that the premises, approximately where we now are centered, could be ours if we wanted them. A small matter to some, but encouragement to those venturing out in faith!

Our circumstances in Edinburgh, however, were quite different from Glasgow. In Pollok, St. James was the only Protestant Church for some 20,000 people, whereas in the Capital, the Grange was one of some half-dozen churches long established in about the same area and population, and, whereas our Glasgow Group was a kind of background brotherhood, the Fellowship was an institution in itself. This raises the question Cameron Peddie felt strongly about. Should Christian Healing be confined to the normal Christian ministry or should it be relegated to a specialised compartment run by enthusiasts? Peddie had a strong case here, for there is little doubt that Jesus Himself so regarded the matter, combining Preaching and Healing, and one has to beware that this special aspect of the faith does not just become a kind of religious side-show. On the other hand, where few churches do in fact practise the ministry where are people to turn if their need is not met locally? Furthermore, such centres are valuable for instruction, encouragement and propagating the faith. God works in different ways in different places and His hand is apparent in both approaches.

But, though it was not possible to develop things along the same lines in both my congregations some of our Grange church members attended our Fellowship meetings, and each Sunday morning we also had a short Service of Healing prior to the ordinary service of worship. Furthermore when leading English and American figures came to speak at our conferences they frequently preached from our pulpit and conferred with people thereafter.

Indeed the Conference aspect of the Fellowship's work was very important. Apart from annual ones of a more local nature we had, with the backing of the Guild of Health, two of an international nature. These were given considerable press coverage and one a Civic Reception. How different in public regard from only a few years previously, when two of us ministers, although strongly encouraged by the Superintendent of one of Glasgow's largest hospitals, were denied use of its chapel by the chaplain for a short private service!

Central to the work in the Fellowship was the Prayer Service with a large number of intercessors and requests from all over the country. When one is told that we are living in a secular and uninterested age, experience working in this sphere soon opens one's eyes to a very different situation. The institutional church might well in days of discouragement be assured that human need was never greater than today and spiritual resource never in short supply.

Healing continued in the new sphere as in the old, though perhaps there was a difference in the nature of the problems we endeavoured to deal with. Mrs Thomas lived in a mining town outside Edinburgh and suffered so acutely from agoraphobia that she feared to leave her house even to shop. However, one day her minister bundled her into his car and took her along to us. She came into the room somewhat timorously, sat down and received the laying-on-of-hands in the usual fashion. When she left I was not aware that any great change had taken place. Actually she went away with all her fears gone and completely cured for ten years. She not only resumed her household duties but took up employment. Sometimes she attended church meetings and bore witness telling how her healing had come. When, after some ten years, some of the symptoms began to return, she called on us once again and after prayer and a service of healing had another five years clear. Thereafter we heard nothing further.

A major case of similar nature was that of Miss Forrest, an elderly, retired school teacher who was unable to walk. She had had a strange upbringing, her father having died when she was very young and her mother being a very dominant, probably nervous character, who demanded much attention. It was probably an invention of the latter that made her tell her daughter that if she should marry before she was twenty she would lose her right to the family fortune! Now, our Miss Forrest was a woman of considerable talents and ambition and as the years passed, she was torn between her duty to her mother and her own fulfilment in her chosen profession. Then she became ill for a period with a good excuse for desisting from the inner conflict, and found a wonderful peace of mind. Later she happened to fall and went through some kind of trauma, after which she could scarcely walk at all and so had finally to retire from her profession. The psychological factors in this case are so obvious as scarcely to need pointing out. Her mother of course had died long since, so that the background situation no longer existed but the sense of guilt remained. She had had psychiatric treatment but her consultant eventually sent her on to us. We assured her of God's deep forgiveness and referred her to Jesus healing the paralytic (Mark 2. vv 1-12) where He did not, to the puzzlement of many, no doubt, in the first place say "Rise up and walk!" but "Thy sins are forgiven". Progress with an elderly woman like Miss Forrest was slow but real, and coming with us on a tour of the Holy Land, she declared it was the best holiday in her life.

However there wasn't anything psychological about the case of Mrs Rhys a native of Berwick-on-Tweed suffering from a disfiguring condition of her nails which was very distressing. She had been visiting a clinic in Newcastle-on-Tyne for ten years without improvement. Then she was transferred to Edinburgh Royal Infirmary when, urged by a friend, she came to us monthly on her visits north. After several months she said one day "My consultant knows you and is a member of your church". This astonished me, until I realised this was an Australian doctor who, with his family, had come to Scotland for a two year course in the study of skin trouble. When I saw him on the following Sunday I mentioned the case of Mrs Rhys, and to my surprise he said rather brusquely, for he was usually very, courteous. "Quite hopeless! The matrix from which the nails grow has been destroyed and recovery is impossible!" Not long after, he and his family having being given a warm farewell, departed to their homeland. But, on Mrs Rhys' next visit, it was obvious that normal nails were growing in after these eleven years. The doctor and I were corresponding and I included the news in my next letter. However in replying he made no reference to Mrs Rhys. I suppose he concluded that his treatment had not been so ineffective as they had supposed. But he was a very religious man and one wonders if in his deepest thought a seed had not been sown.

Though it is true that at the congregational level the Healing Ministry is natural and personal the Fellowship should widen one's outlook. Once I was present when the sympathetic Superintendent of a large hospital in the south of Scotland said privately to Cameron Peddie, who had been asked to tell of his experiences to the medical staff, "Don't make it too easy!" This is a hint that should be taken by all groups inclined to be too turned in upon themselves. With the Fellowship contact with organisations like the Churches Council of Healing, composed equally of medicals and church people helped us to have critical minds ourselves and also to be open to other approaches. Denominational differences we tended to let lapse and with the Episcopalians in particular our links became very close. One of their most distinguished Bishops chaired the main part of one of our conferences and brought with him, as a speaker, one of his members who claimed special healing gifts. And thereby hangs a tale.

Several Sundays before the start of one of our Conferences which had had a good deal of publicity, I had a call from the Telephone Samaritans saying they had been approached by a family in the Borders with a boy of 12 years of age who had had foot surgery followed by constant pain necessitating his absence from school for several months. Ordinary medical treatment had not been successful in alleviating the pain and they wondered if it would be worth their while making the long journey to Edinburgh in their search for a cure. This indeed presented me with a dilemma. We weren't miracle workers in the ordinary sense, and yet here we were holding a Conference purposing to do just this very thing - so I said "Yes! Invite them to come on Wednesday afternoon when we will be holding a Healing service!"

When Wednesday afternoon came we had large numbers seeking help so we had to allocate to them, and those ministering to them, different rooms. Personally I was not very sure of the Bishop's psychic friend so decided that he and I would work together, I myself offering the prayers. Last on the list was our stricken boy who had come on crutches. I began the service but had to leave because I was due to take the chair at the next public meeting. At five o'clock when this had concluded, I learned that in the meantime the boy had abandoned his crutches and left the building cured. The following Saturday he was sharing in the dancing at his sister's wedding and years later I was informed that he grew to be a policeman, six feet two in height. From this I learned several lessons. Always accept the challenge to one's faith and keep an open mind as to whom God is willing to help, and how!

One day when I was still in Pollok, there phoned my house a Jewish business man desperately seeking healing. I asked him to come and see me and we agreed that for the next month he should twice a week receive Divine Healing. His trouble was depression. It had been with him all his life and he thought his mother must have been depressed before he was born. Latterly the condition had got deeper and more severe. When I ministered to him, for reasons of courtesy I concentrated more on Old Testament references than New, though within I sought the help of the great Christian Healer. At the end of the period he showed little improvement, or appreciation, and I was somewhat relieved that the episode was over. Indeed I saw him no more but six weeks later he telephoned my house in my absence, leaving a message. Please to tell the minister that his sense of depression had lifted. He had never felt so well in his life, and kindly to thank him for what he had done. What are we to make of a story like this? There was so little between us. He was not an attractive man, his trouble was deep and we did not even share a common faith. Yet here he was, not just cured, but full of gratitude he had taken the trouble to express. As the old hymn has it "There's a wideness in God's mercy like the wideness of the sea".

APPROACHES TO HEALING
THE MEDICAL WORLD

H.G. Wells once wrote that the greatest blessing conferred on mankind was the discovery of anaesthetics last century, and if one considers the amount of pain suffered by human beings in previous ages this is surely true. Since then medical science has leapt forward in great strides so that the knowledge and experience accumulated should be regarded both with great respect and gratitude. Therefore we, engaged in the spiritual aspect, should value the opinion of the physician in the various situations in which we find ourselves. In my early days, I personally appreciated greatly, contact with a local doctor who would advise me if his treatment of a patient was being altered. Doctors are well aware that in most cases there is a psychological element. The doctor tends to treat not just an illness but a patient. What suits one person is not necessarily the cure for another.

Not that we should think that the psychological factor is to be taken as something of no great value in itself. Once a well-known figure who practised Healing, visiting churches all round the country, had the use of St. James. After a religious service he simply assured the sick that they were cured. As he pointed to one of my church members, who was seriously ill with sinusitis, the lady immediately felt her head clear. So it continued for the next six months. Suppose one does write this off as psychological, one asks "What did happen?" Would not a pill which achieved this result be considered quite real and effective? There is in fact a whole world here, of which not the wisest of us, knows very much at all. Many leading physicians have on such matters a very open mind and I have heard the Superintendent of one of Glasgow's largest hospitals say about a case dealt with successfully by Cameron Peddie "This is the most extraordinary thing I have seen."

My father in his later years was in hospital with prostate trouble and such severe haemorrhage that I was informed his life was in danger, since surgery was in these conditions impossible. I therefore asked whether it would be permissible to have Mr Peddie minister to him, and was informed that this was quite acceptable. That same evening I took the latter with me and the service was given. Next afternoon when I called to see my father it was to find that not only had the bleeding stopped but the operation had been undertaken. However, not surprisingly, the bleeding recommenced after the operation and continued so persistently that the patient's life was seriously threatened. Once again Peddie's help was sought and within a short period of time the flow was completely staunched and recovery ensued. A week later, I was joined in the hospital corridor by one of the medicals who commented "Well, your friend fairly did it!" Rather surprised I said "Oh, were you watching what what was going on?" and he laughed "Oh, we were all watching very keenly for we had done all we could without avail. Then your friend came along and the bleeding stopped. Then the second time we again failed and again, almost immediately, your friend succeeded!" It is right to give the scientific approach priority but it is encouraging to know that the physician often realises that there is another dimension and is sympathetic to approaches other than his own.

Some years ago I met a young man whose professional future was threatened owing to fits of panic which overcame him from time to time. After we had several meetings the trouble completely disappeared for we had been able to unearth a period of considerable stress in his childhood. I remarked "How easy it is to help when you know a little about psychiatry!" but he responded "Oh, no! It was your prayers that did it!" Probably there was truth in both verdicts. Science can unearth Causes, but faith is the great Healer.

THE THEOLOGICAL ASPECT

Today many church people talk glibly of Divine Healing - but what do we mean by the term? Even our theologically minded are not very helpful here. Does it just mean that God answers prayer and acts purely by spiritual means? - or is there some kind of material force called into being? A good deal of the way we practise the ministry will depend on this.

The reader will realise that my own experience has been along the line of the latter approach. In Glasgow we were largely guided by Cameron Peddie. While he could truly be called the most self-giving of men, he was not much of a theologian nor did he have a very critical mind. But, of his entire commitment there can be no doubt, nor of the fact that he was truly in touch with a spiritual dimension unexplored by the average Christian. He believed that the healing power of the New Testament was something more than a prayer for the sick, which is why he called his book "The Forgotten Talent". As far as he expressed his opinion in the matter, he favoured the full exercise of the ministry being confined chiefly to the ordained. The Gospels, the Book of Acts and the Epistles of St Paul (cp I Corinthians 12.30) lend some substance to this point of view.

There are two other factors one could take into consideration. The first is the reactions which numbers of people seem to have after the laying-on-of-hands. Personally I feel this is more than "psychological". The other reason is a suggestion which has come my way in practising the ministry is that there could be in it some kind of apostolic succession.

Once, two of us in the Glasgow Group were called to relieve an elderly man suffering severely in a painful illness. Our ministration seemed to help him greatly and he said "Oh, if I had known sooner that ministers could do this!" I returned later on my own and his whole condition was much improved until, having myself caught a cold, I phoned another of our Group and asked him to take my place. This he was most reluctant to do, for among his own people he seemed to have no success. However he was eventually persuaded and next day informed me, very happily, that not only had the patient been helped, but when he himself had been conducting his weekly Service of Healing people had responded as never before. This made me wonder whether the sick man had not received something from previous ministrations leading back to the special resources so evident in Peddie, which had been passed on, and opened channels previously closed. On another occasion having gone forward myself to receive the laying-on-of-hands from one very much involved in the Movement, as I felt very inadequate for the programmes immediately ahead, there certainly was given an upsurge of power. Two days later, a business man laid up in bed was able to get up and return to work, and an old lady suffering severely from shingles was relieved immediately, and, to the best of my knowledge, (she was a member of my own family) never complained again.

These personal experiences confirmed my belief that there is in the Healing gift something distinctive. Ralph Morton, deputy leader of the Iona Community in its first days used to say that in Healing, love was as important as faith. St Paul declared that "though I have all faith so that I could remove mountains and have not love, I am nothing." This no doubt is true but, however skilful and caring, a surgeon still needs his tools. In Presbyterian Churches though ordination is indeed not regarded as a sacrament and is never administered by one person alone, yet its special significance is safe-guarded by the fact that those taking part are themselves ordained. I have already borne tribute to the tremendous part congregations as a body can play in Healing but I would like there to be, in church order, a place reserved so that people in need may know that, if there is indeed a special gift, those ministering are commissioned to its exercise.

THE SOCIAL ASPECT

It is notable that a couple of generations after Bible times the Healing Ministry in the Church tended to decline. Was this because some of its tenets had become more formal? Even if so, however, all was not lost. Early in the second century Christians built the first hospital of which we have record, and surely that was a great step forward.

Is it not important to consider practical and social factors? Prayers alone are not much use in feeding the hungry, and throughout our modern prosperous world there are multitudes of people on the verge of starvation. There are indeed many tragic cases round our doors. Twenty-five years ago there came to the Fellowship a youth, fresh and attractive. In boyhood he had met with an accident and he believed his brain had been damaged. We got on well with him but he did not make the progress hoped for. I interviewed the hospital psychiatrist but what he said was "Keep him off the drink!" In this, despite our efforts, we failed to succeed. Nowadays I meet him almost weekly and sometimes buy him a meal. But, slouching along, bent and unkempt, he is distressing to look on. Can we blame him living in a society where every few yards he passes shops displaying the alcohol which has destroyed him? The trouble with modern society is not that we have too little, but that we have too much. The opportunity we have for more indulgent living often leads not to more happiness but to more broken homes and broken hearts. We have to be concerned not only with healing but with causes. "Don't make things too easy!" said the doctor to Cameron Peddie and it could be that we should apply this to ourselves in exercising simpler lifestyles.

CHRIST THE HEALER

In recent years as the statistics of the various Churches come in they make depressing reading. Possibly we ourselves privately may have the feeling that the church is not so relevant to our lives as it could be. Yet, within the Healing Movement the whole ethos tends to be so different. Human need is as great as ever and there is no falling off in those seeking help. Furthermore, there is a much wider range both in the subject itself and those prepared to help in providing it. For many years now we have bodies committed to the ministry like Iona with Healing at its centre, individuals like George Fox and others venturing out in faith, and the Groups and Fellowships we have been describing, feeling not decline but strength for the present and hope of greater things yet to be.

Such know that the Gospel has all the power it always had. While in rapidly changing times theology may wobble, from the beginning authentic Christian faith has dealt primarily not so much with ideas as with people. The New Testament is a record of how *people* have had their problems solved. Lives healed are the most powerful sermons preached and Christian Healing should be the healing of the whole man.

Examples of this are around us every day, but I think the most interesting story I know is located in India where the late Dr Jack Drummond for many years exercised a wonderful ministry before returning to this country, when we got to know him well as a member of the Fellowship.

The tale he had to tell was that, one day there appeared at his mission station a paralysed youth who, unable to walk, had, for many miles and over several days, made the journey from his home swinging along resting on his hands. Desperately seeking help, he possibly had thought that Drummond was a medical doctor, but Jack, a Doctor of Divinity, assured him that that was not so, and that what he ought to do was to pray to God, as Jesus was the Great Healer. The mission people cared for the lad and saw to it that he was conveyed comfortably back to his own village.

Dr Drummond thereafter departed on furlough, but, on his return, when visiting in the country, decided, though it was some miles away, to look in on the boy's village. On his way, he asked a man in a field if he knew the lad and what his condition now was. When the man said he was in good health, but would not have returned from his work by the time the missionary had reached the village, the latter said they could not be thinking of the same person. But, indeed, this turned out to be the truth, and when, later in the day, the youth did appear Dr Drummond expressed his delighted surprise at his recovery. But then it was the boy's turn to be surprised: "Why do you think it strange? It was you who told me to pray to Jesus for healing. I did so and He healed me!"

There is food for thought here. We use words but do we always mean them? Here it is the teacher who is taught the lesson.

He was to learn another when, next day, he passed on to another village which previously had always rebuffed him. This time he was not only made welcome but invited to deliver the Christian message. In due course he asked the village head whether the healing of the young man had been the cause of the change of attitude. "Oh no!" came the reply. "Our own gods can cure the sick. What has impressed us has been the change in the boy's father. Before, he was one of the most evil men you could find. Nowadays he is completely altered and become one of the best.

Lesser gods can heal the sick but a God who can make a bad man good is a God worth knowing about."

Perhaps here we have the deepest truth of all. Christian Healing permeates all life, body, mind and character. The pity is when people get hold of only one aspect and think they have all. Of course the implication is that behind all there is great power which throws us back on the source of all good, God himself. But this, in turn, should be our encouragement, for it means we are not dependent on our own resources.

Having done our own part we must leave the rest to the One we all regard as the greatest Healer of all. I think of the verse our choir at St James' used to sing at the close of the Intercessory Service:

>The healing of His seamless dress
>Is by our beds of pain.
>We touch Him in life's throng and press
>And we are whole again.